What Are Shadows and Reflections?

Robin Johnson

 Crabtree Publishing Company
www.crabtreebooks.com

Author
Robin Johnson

Publishing plan research and development
Reagan Miller

Editorial director
Kathy Middleton

Editor
Kathy Middleton

Proofreader
Shannon Welbourn

Design
Samara Parent

Photo research
Samara Parent

Production coordinator
and prepress technician
Samara Parent

Print coordinator
Margaret Amy Salter

Photographs
Thinkstock: pages 5, 7 (bottom middle and right),
12, 14, 15 (top right), 17
All other images by Shutterstock

Library and Archives Canada Cataloguing in Publication

Johnson, Robin (Robin R.), author
    What are shadows and reflections? / Robin Johnson.

(Light and sound waves close-up)
Includes index.
Issued in print and electronic formats.
ISBN 978-0-7787-0521-5 (bound).--ISBN 978-0-7787-0525-3 (pbk.).--
ISBN 978-1-4271-9010-9 (html).--ISBN 978-1-4271-9014-7 (pdf)

    1. Reflection (Optics)--Juvenile literature. 2. Shades and
shadows--Juvenile literature. 3. Light--Juvenile literature.
I. Title.

QC425.2.J64 2014   j535   C2014-900809-0
                                         C2014-900810-4

Library of Congress Cataloging-in-Publication Data

Johnson, Robin (Robin R.), author.
  What are shadows and reflections? / Robin Johnson.
      pages cm -- (Light and sound waves close-up)
  Includes index.
   ISBN 978-0-7787-0521-5 (reinforced library binding) --
 ISBN 978-0-7787-0525-3 (pbk.) --
 ISBN 978-1-4271-9014-7 (electronic pdf) --
 ISBN 978-1-4271-9010-9 (electronic html)
 1. Reflection (Optics)--Juvenile literature. 2. Shades and shadows--Juvenile
literature. 3. Light--Juvenile literature. I. Title.

 QC425.2.J64 2014
 535'.323--dc23   2014004279

Crabtree Publishing Company

www.crabtreebooks.com   1-800-387-7650

Printed in Canada/082017/MQ20170616

Published in Canada
Crabtree Publishing
616 Welland Ave.
St. Catharines, Ontario
L2M 5V6

Published in the United States
Crabtree Publishing
PMB 59051
350 Fifth Avenue, 59th Floor
New York, New York 10118

Published in the United Kingdom
Crabtree Publishing
Maritime House
Basin Road North, Hove
BN41 1WR

Published in Australia
Crabtree Publishing
3 Charles Street
Coburg North
VIC 3058

Contents

What is light?

Light is the brightness that shows you the world around you. It lets you see the butterflies and flowers outside. Light lets you play with your cars and trains inside your house. It helps you find treasures in caves and other dark places. Light really brightens up your day!

Without light to see, we would have to rely on our other senses to figure out our world.

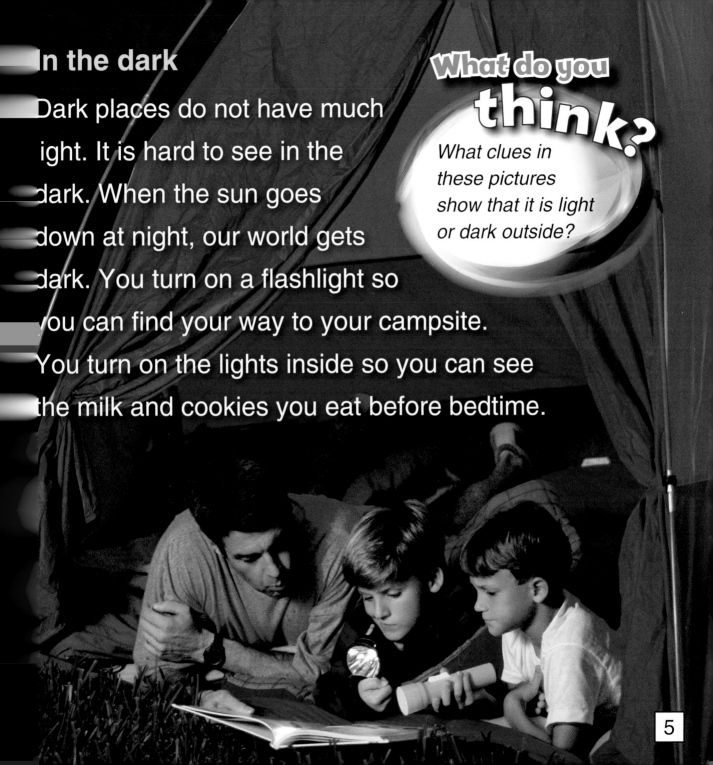

In the dark

Dark places do not have much light. It is hard to see in the dark. When the sun goes down at night, our world gets dark. You turn on a flashlight so you can find your way to your campsite. You turn on the lights inside so you can see the milk and cookies you eat before bedtime.

What do you think?

What clues in these pictures show that it is light or dark outside?

Where does light come from?

There are many **sources** of light. A source is the place where something comes from. The main source of light on Earth is the sun. The sun is a huge ball of hot gas in the sky. Its light shines down on the entire world. It gives light and heat to all living things.

Shining lights

Light bulbs are another source of light. When you turn on a light in your home, a light bulb **glows**. The light bulb helps you find the flashlight you need for your camping trip. The flashlight helps you get wood in the forest to make a campfire. The fire is a source of light, too!

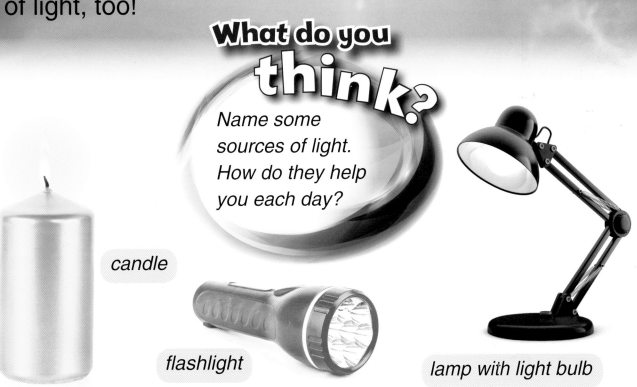

What do you think?

Name some sources of light. How do they help you each day?

candle

flashlight

lamp with light bulb

Light waves

All light sources make **light waves**. Light waves are rays, or beams of **energy**, that our eyes see as the colors of the rainbow. When we see all the colors together, light appears white. Light waves travel quickly from their source. They move in straight lines until they meet up with **matter**. Everything is made up of matter. Matter is anything you can see or touch.

rainbow

| red |
| orange |
| yellow |
| green |
| blue |
| indigo |
| violet |

Soak it up

When light waves meet matter, the matter **absorbs** some of the light. To absorb is to soak up. For example, a red wagon is red, because the wagon absorbs all the colors in the light waves except red. The color red is not soaked up, so we see it on the wagon.

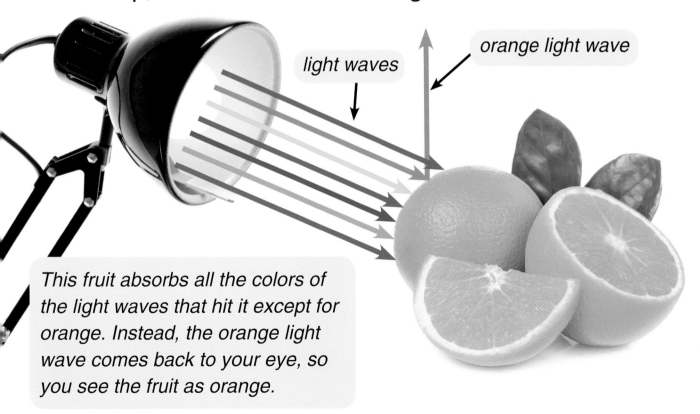

light waves

orange light wave

This fruit absorbs all the colors of the light waves that hit it except for orange. Instead, the orange light wave comes back to your eye, so you see the fruit as orange.

Light bounces

When light hits matter, the matter **reflects** some of the energy in the light waves. To reflect is to bounce off something. The light bounces from object to object and right into your eyes! Bouncing light waves let you see the world around you.

Not all things that shine are light sources. The moon lights up the world at night, but it is not a source of light. Light from the sun hits the moon and makes the moon shine at night. The moon reflects the light from the sun down to Earth.

Mirrors reflect

A mirror reflects your smiling face! It can also be used to change the path of light. When a beam of light hits the shiny surface of a mirror, the light reflects off it. When you move the mirror, it changes the direction in which the light beam travels.

Light bends

Matter also **refracts** light. To refract is to bend or change the direction of something. Light travels through air, water, and other matter. Light waves bend when they move from one type of matter into another. Different types of matter make light waves bend in different ways.

Refraction can play tricks on your eyes! This boy in the pool looks closer under water and farther away in the air above the water.

Light magic

Try this simple test to bend light waves. Pour some water into a glass. Put a straw or other straight object into the water. Look at it from the side. The straw will look like it is in two pieces. It is not a magic trick! Light bends when it moves from the water to the air.

A diamond gets its sparkle from light bouncing off and passing through it. Light that goes through it is broken up and sent in many different directions.

A clear matter

Light can travel through air and water because they are **transparent**. Transparent matter lets light pass through it. It does not block light. Windows are also transparent. The sun streams through your window and shines on your face.

Cats like to take naps in the warm sunlight that shines through windows.

Not so clear

Other matter blocks some of the light and lets some light move through it. Matter that allows some light to pass through is called **translucent**. Plastic milk jugs are translucent. You can tell that there is milk inside the jug but you cannot see the milk clearly.

balloons

milk in jug

Stained glass has both transparent and translucent glass.

motor oil

What do you think?

Some liquids are translucent such as oil for your car. Can you think of some translucent liquids that you eat?

Blocking light

Some matter blocks the light. No light can pass through it at all. Matter that blocks light is called **opaque**. Many of the things you see around you are opaque. Walls and wooden doors are opaque. Tables and chairs are opaque. You are opaque, too!

The door and wall are opaque. The only light that gets through is from the small opening between them.

Making shadows

When light hits an opaque object, the object blocks the light. Blocking the light makes a dark area behind the object where the light cannot reach. This dark area is called a **shadow**.

What do you think?

Look at the objects around you. Are they opaque? Or can you see through them?

Sun and shadows

The sun makes shadows on Earth. It shines down from the sky and lights the world. When trees, houses, and other matter block the sunlight, shadows are formed. Without the sun, we would not have shadows!

light from the sun

shadow

On the move

Your body blocks the sun and creates shadows all around you. When the sun shines in front of you, you see a shadow behind you. When the sun shines behind you, you see a shadow in front of you. Shadows move and change as you run and play in the sunshine.

What do you think?

What do you need to make a shadow?

If you stood outside in one place for several hours, your shadow would move. This happens because the sun's position above you changes during the day.

Light it up!

Follow these steps to see how light passes through different objects. You will see light waves in a whole new light!

Materials:

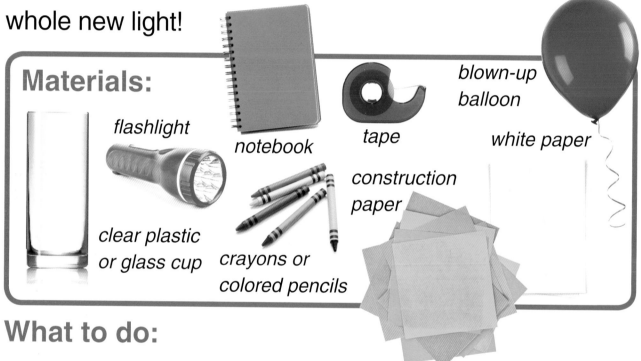

flashlight

notebook

tape

blown-up balloon

white paper

construction paper

clear plastic or glass cup

crayons or colored pencils

What to do:

1. Tape the white paper to a wall.

2. Shine the flashlight onto the paper. Look at the circle of light. Draw what you see in a notebook.

3. Now place one of the objects between the flashlight and the paper. Look at the circle of light again. How has it changed? Is it more or less bright? Draw what you see.

4. Do it again with other objects. Try to **predict** if the objects will let light pass through them or not. To predict is to tell something before it takes place.

See the light!

Look at your drawings. You will see that light acts in different ways when it meets different kinds of matter. Group the objects by how much light passes through them. Are they transparent, translucent, or opaque? Did you predict the light correctly?

What do you think?

What happens when you block the light with an opaque object? What appears on the wall?

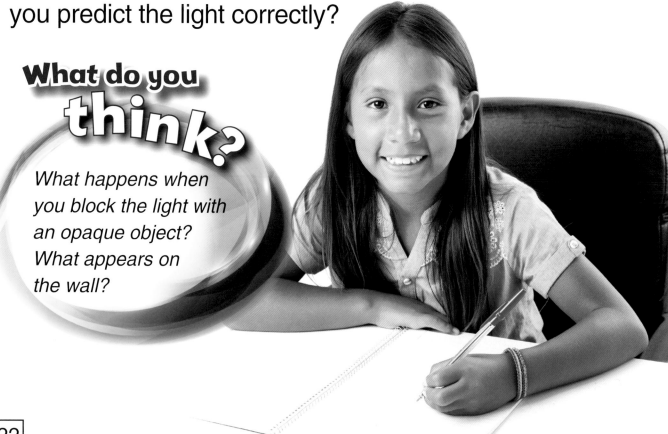

Learning More

Books

Amazing Light by Sally Hewitt. Crabtree Publishing Company, 2007.

Follow It!: Learn About Shadows by Pamela Hall. Child's World, 2010.

Light & Dark by Wendy Madgwick. Armadillo, 2014.

Light: Shadows, Mirrors, and Rainbows by Natalie M. Rosinsky. Picture Window Books, 2002.

Light Show: Reflection and Absorption by Jack Torrence. PowerKids Press, 2009.

Shadows and Reflections by Daniel Nunn. Heinemann-Raintree, 2012.

Websites

Easy Science for Kids: All About Light and Dark
http://easyscienceforkids.com/all-about-light-and-dark/

Optics for Kids
www.optics4kids.org/home/

Science Kids: Light for Kids
www.sciencekids.co.nz/light.html

Words to know

absorb (ab-SAWRB) *verb* To soak up

energy (EN-er-jee) *noun* The power to do work

glow (gloh) *verb* To give off light

light wave (lahyt weyv) *noun* A ray of energy you see as the colors of the rainbow

matter (MAT-er) *noun* Something that takes up space

opaque (oh-PEYK) *adjective* Does not allow light to pass through

predict (pri-DIKT) *verb* To tell something before it takes place

reflect (ri-FLEKT) *verb* To bounce off something

refract (ri-FRAKT) *verb* To bend or change the direction of something

shadow (SHAD-oh) *noun* A dark shape made when an object blocks the light

source (sohrs) *noun* The place where something begins or comes from

translucent (trans-LOO-suh nt) *adjective* Lets some light pass through

transparent (trans-PAIR-uh nt) *adjective* Lets light pass through

A noun is a person, place, or thing. An adjective is a word that tells you what something is like. A verb is an action word that tells you what someone or something does.

Index